LEADERSHIP UNDER 30

MAXIMS FOR YOUNG LEADERS

Frederick O. Towles

Leadership Under 30: Maxims For Young Leaders

Frederick O. Towles

© 2014 First Love Media

First Love Media is an imprint of NiOse Group, LLC

ISBN 978-0-692-29989-0

Printed in the United States of America

Introduction

One of the most frightening things as a young leader is coming to grips with the fact that you are actually leading a team of people – whether it be a small group, a company, grassroots non-profit organization or even a family.

I have personally been in a leadership role throughout my 20's and 30's. My colleagues and I, at the time felt the same way. We were glad for the opportunity to lead but at times felt slightly overwhelmed with the responsibility.

Leadership is an awesome assignment that can become overwhelming at times. In fact King Solomon when asked what he needed, Solomon asked for the ability to distinguish between right and wrong and the ability to govern the people whom he was not king over. Simply put, Solomon asked for divine help in leadership.

That is how important leadership is. John Maxwell once said that 'everything rises and falls on leadership."

In this book, I would like to share some maxims that I have learned over the years which have helped me become a better leader.

My hope is that through reading this book, you will find some level of inspiration and encouragement. The areas that you are leading each need a better "you." These maxims can help you continue on the path to being better. Happy reading and happy learning!

Dedications and Acknowledgements

I would like to dedicate this book to my loving wife, Latishia. She has been there with me for a long time. Just want to say I love you!

I also want to dedicate this to my mentors over the years: Mr. Darren Moore, Rev. Curtis Thompson, the late Rev. Gene McGhee, the late Dr. Roderick Caesar Sr., Dr. Roderick Caesar Jr., Mr. Mark Smith, Rev. Keith Boswell, the late Mr. Mack Logan, Dr. Carlo, Mr. Edwin Thompson, Mr. John Roth, Rev. Willie McGhee, Mr. Lawrence J. Cormier, the late Mr. Charles A. Pringle Jr., Esq., Rev. Alan Plummer Jr., Dr. Larry Acosta, Freddie L. Towles (my Dad), Rev. James Towles, Mr. Cornelius Towles and a host of others that have impacted my life.

Thank you NiOse Group LLC and Unlimited Expectations Inc. for your work on this book.

Maxim #1
Identify and develop other leaders

The lifeblood of any organization, company or team is its ability to develop other leaders. This is something that cannot be forsaken or it will literally kill the group over a period of time.

As time passes, people and ideas get older. As much as we would like to deny it, if we aren't careful, leaders can become complacent – unwilling to take risks, unwilling to train, stuck in an obsolete leadership model or satisfied with the success that has been achieved on their watch.

In order to thwart these types of complacency that await you as a leader, you must find other leaders to join your leadership team. In order to identify potential leaders within your organization you must be observant.

While observing, you should ask yourself and your current leadership team some key questions. Some of these questions are: Who seems to have the mission of the organization, company, or team on their hearts? Who do the members of the team organically seem to gravitate to? Is there someone in the organization showing leadership potential?

There will be a number of people to whom you will be able to answer each of those questions affirmatively. This does not in any way earmark them as leaders. But it does get your organization thinking in the right direction. By doing this, you have formed what I like to call a leadership funnel.

Once you have identified potential leaders within the organization, you will need to form some level of leadership development program. There are a number of leadership development programs currently on the market. If you choose to develop your own, so be it. However, there are two leadership programs that may peak your interest: The Ken Blanchard Companies and Dale Carnegie Training.

The more you develop the leadership team and the leaders that make up the team, the more your organization has a chance to work at its optimal level. Remember: undeveloped leaders and/or an undeveloped leadership team will cause chaos within the organization over time.

Maxim #2
Maintain your integrity

Being faithful and true to what you said you would do and who you say you are may by far be the most important personal maxim in this book.

You should be known inside and outside of your organization as a person of integrity. When it comes to moral issues and following the principles of the organization you should never fall into question. This can only occur when you practice being faithful to what you say.

At times, things come up which can make it virtually impossible for you to execute what you said you would do. If that is the case, own it and make sure that your team or organization knows the extenuating circumstances that prevent you from executing your plan.

There are two examples of what can prevent you from

executing your plan: family emergencies and poor planning.

Family emergencies or other emergencies are bound to happen at times. These emergencies come without warning and many have to be addressed immediately. Poor planning can and should be addressed. Poor planning is revealed in a number of ways: being overwhelmed by projects, distractions - not prioritizing, and oversight. Whatever causes a delay in executing your plan, own it and let your team know what's going on.

Being a person of integrity also doesn't mean you won't make mistakes from time to time; you're human. Own what you did; don't hide in the darkness.

Remember, leadership is like a relationship. In a relationship when trust is broken, the relationship is ruined. In like manner, when a leader's integrity is proven faulty, trust is broken and it can send devastating rippling effects throughout the group you lead.

When you own your mistakes or inability to execute, it will help buffer your integrity and could prevent a traumatizing effect on your group.

Maxim #3
Never make rash decisions in the moment

Making rash decisions in the heat of the moment is an absolute recipe for disaster. There are times in the heat of the moment when you will need to make a decision, but try not to make any harsh ones.

As much as possible, step away from the situation, evaluate all the stakeholders affected by the situation and all of the possible outcomes then make your decision.

When you can't take a step back before making a decision, remain calm, work through the evaluations and outcomes, but don't be afraid to request some time to make the decision. Just because you are the leader, you don't have to have all the answers instantly.

A brief moment to evaluate stakeholders and calibrate outcomes could keep key people on the team and avoid unnecessary conflicts.

Maxim #4
Find out what keeps your emotional tank full

Leadership can be a lonely road filled with misunderstandings, difficult decisions, investments of time and resources and a host of other complexities. If you are married, have children, are a student or engaged in a career you will find these can be a part of the other complexities faced on your leadership journey.

All of this can be very demanding and draining. The demand made on leaders can cause depression and anxiety, if not checked. Because of this, it is important to know what gets your emotional tank full.

What do you do that causes excitement? What hobby do you like to engage in? When you have some "down time" what are you naturally drawn to? These are just a few questions that can unlock the answer to what fills your emotional tank. As long as the activity isn't illegal or unethical you want to carve out some time in your schedule to engage in it.

I once heard a story from a person in a leadership role who was feeling some level of anxiety. This anxiety was birthed from the constant grind of engaging in his leadership role without a break.

One day he decided to take a break and catch two or three movies at a theater. Going to the movies was the activity that helped replenish his emotional tank. Ironically, a few moments after exiting the theater he received a call alerting him of an emergency situation.

He expressed his gratitude for being able to fill his emotional tank. This allowed him to have the right mental state in order to handle the emergency.

When our emotional tank isn't full we have the tendency to react incorrectly to situations by either running away or making rash decisions. Some leaders have even committed suicide when facing situations without their emotional tank being full.

Think of your emotional tank like the gas tank of a car. When the gas tank is full, the vehicle works at its optimal capacity. When the tank begins to get low there are indicators to alert the driver that gas is needed. If the driver decides not to replenish the tank, at some point the car will stop functioning at its optimal capacity.

You and I are the same way. Let's play close attention to our indicators and respond accordingly.

Maxim #5
Never complain about the people who are working with you

Language is everything, so be very careful what you say and how you say it. One of the worse things that you can do is complain. Far worse than that, you should never complain about a person on your team. Complaining about someone on your team can cause divisions within the team. It can also make you appear to others on the team as one who isn't fit for leadership.

There are going to be some situations when you will be upset with someone on your team because they didn't execute properly. But this is not a cause to complain about it to anyone. Instead of complaining, try to take the "high road." Here is what that looks like. Remember, you always have options.

First, if something goes on in your organization that may cause you to complain, don't see it as a chance to complain, see it as an opportunity for growth. Conflict, from time to time, is necessary in the growth process.

Second, always try to see things from the other person's point of view. Ask yourself, "Was the person given the proper instruction?" Did someone follow up with the person to ensure that progress was being made? Were you too busy with performing another set of tasks and couldn't communicate the instructions? Do you give off a friendly and inviting persona or one of intimidation and fear? You may find that someone on your team isn't equipped well enough to execute a given task.

Third, speak to the person who didn't execute properly to find out the details regarding the situation. Don't go into this meeting on the attack, be calm and hear the team member out.

Complaining is tempting at times but it typically does more harm than good for the group you lead.

Maxim #6
Build a culture of unity

We must eliminate the use of "I" and "them" rather use "we" and "us".

Unity causes an organization to thrive. There is nothing more debilitating to the unity of a group than to have its members think individual first ("I" and "them") rather than team ("we" and "us").

The team is always greater than an individual. It has been said that on all sports teams, the team name appears on the front of the uniform and the players name is on the back because the team is bigger than the individual player. If you think team first as a leader, you will heighten your chances to experience success.

Maxim #7
Build a culture of openness

The essence of this maxim is to be open to critique from your peers and the members of your team. The secondary point for this maxim is to be approachable.

With all of the degrees and years of experience many leaders have, this maxim may be the most valuable.

No one wants to be led by a dictator or a tyrant. At the same time, no one who is productive wants to be led by someone who has no standards. Therefore, leaders must possess a sense of openness.

Here is what I mean by openness. Leaders should give space to those they work with to express constructive criticism regarding how the organization is executing or planning. Constructive criticism is healthy for a good leader and a good organization.

Winston Churchill once said, "Criticism may not be agreeable, but it is necessary. It fulfills the same function as pain in the human body. It calls attention to an unhealthy state of things." Churchill hit it on the head. We might not want to hear the critique of others but their critique typically points out weak points in our leadership ability, character and the organization we lend leadership to.

Therefore we must build a culture within our organizations or teams that is open to hear the critique of others without feeling personally attacked.

The second point is that leaders must be approachable. We all give off non-verbal communication that others tend to interpret and develop their conclusions about us. There is no way to undo this, but we can assist those who work with us to consider us approachable.

First, we must be relevant to the times we are leading and living in. I don't mean you must change how you dress or the music you listen to. However, you do need to be aware of the music and trends of the day.

Second, try to listen twice as much as you speak. Leaders should always be learners (we go into this more a little later). People want to know that you care about them and you hear them. When the members of your organization understand that you are willing to listen they will slowly but surely see you as approachable.

Please be aware of time abusers. These are people that just want to talk for the sake of talking.

This leads to the third component of being approachable and that is: consider your time. When someone wants to speak with me about something they will ask me: "Do you have a minute?" My answer to that question is a frank "yes" or "no".

If my answer is "no" I always ask if we can speak about it later and we set a time to talk unless it's very important.

If the answer is "no" but I can probably fit it in, I will alert the person that I have a certain amount of time to talk right then. If the conversation needs more time than that, we will need to schedule it for another time. If the answer is "yes," my response to the person is: "I have a few moments." In either of these cases, you haven't disregarded their need to communicate with you, instead you have remained open to communicate with them.

The fourth and final component is to be available. Never be so busy that you never have time to communicate. If you have the ability, free up some time to communicate with others. Remember the world doesn't revolve around you, even if you think it does.

When you build a culture of openness inside your team or organization it will do wonders for morale and productivity.

Maxim #8
Build a culture of growth

You must challenge your team to grow. An organization or team that isn't growing is probably diminishing. A diminishing team won't be productive and won't last long. How do you get your team to grow?

You as the leader must grow. Don't sit back and rest on your accomplishments. You should always seek to learn and grow.

Encourage growth within your organization by creating opportunities for growth within your organization. This can be done by bringing a professional in to train your team in a particular area that is directly or indirectly related to the field or industry your team operates in.

You can also send members of your team out to local, regional or national trainings directly or indirectly related to your field or industry.

Encourage the reading of personal development books by the members of your team. Perhaps you can offer a suggested reading list of personal development books for the members of your team. While reading won't guarantee growth, it can potentially inspire the reader to grow.

Don't be afraid of your team's growth. I have worked with a great deal of insecure leaders with marginal teams. You don't want that! You want your team members to flourish. Please be aware that this may lead to some of these members leaving at some point. That's fine!

Their departure from your team may also encourage others on the team to grow as well.

Maxim #9
Know that your organization or team will grow to the level that the leader is developed

Houseplants at some point need to be re-potted otherwise they will die. This occurs, from what I have learned, when the plant's roots don't have the adequate space to grow. In like manner, within your organization you have to give the members room to grow. The best way to do this is for you as the leader to grow as well.

As a leader, it is easy to get lost in the operation of the organization. But you must take some time to relax and read to expand your horizons. You must also take time to associate with other people. Remember the world is larger than you and your organization. There are a ton of things out there to learn, experience and grow from. But you won't grow unless you pick your head up from the day-to-day operations of leading your organization, breathe and live.

Don't feel guilty; you are entitled to it every once in a while. Your team will benefit from your experience and so will you. The more you grow the more your team will have the ability and opportunity to grow. You set the tone of your organization.

Maxim #10
Never underestimate or overestimate your team

While looking to optimize the workflow and effectiveness of your team in the name of production, it is easy to lose sight that each team member's capacity to function is different.

Your team is filled with intangibles that don't show themselves on an individual's resume or social media profile. One of your jobs as the leader is to discover some of these intangibles because they may cause your team to operate in a more efficient manner.

What I have realized over the past two decades of leadership is that you never want to expect too much from anyone and you never want to write anyone off.

I once reviewed the profile of a young man who I wanted on my team. His profile was filled with good things that answered every question about if he could "get it done" for us. So I selected him, figuring that he would deliver as promised.

When I met him personally, he had the stature of one who could "get it done" for us. Upon further review, sad to say, I was grossly incorrect. I placed a great deal of value on him in a very vital area and he didn't deliver.

Meanwhile, there was someone else on the team whose profile didn't seem like a good fit but became one of the key people on the team. In fact, he was a leader that I was unaware of. He brought a level of commitment to the organization that quickly ran through the fiber of each member. This gentleman's impact helped the team overcome the letdown caused by my bad decision.

The conclusion here is to get to know everyone, discover their intangibles and never underestimate or overestimate the members of your team.

Maxim #11
Your team will duplicate what you do whether they see it or not

I once led a particular team within a non-profit organization. While leading the team, there was an issue with volunteers showing up when they agreed to show up. (If you have ever worked in a non-profit organization I am sure you have your own stories about volunteers and showing up). So I figured that I would continue to state the mission of the organization and how each of the commitments to this mission would propel the organization to its goal.

As the leader, I thought I would lead by example and be present when I said I would be present. This went well for about seven months. Then one day I had to push off my commitment really for no good reason. Once this occurred I began to see the number of people who didn't show when they said they would increase sharply.

Because you set the tone for the group, your attitude and your behavior mean a lot. Whatever you produce within the organization will be duplicated by your team. It always seems that the bad stuff is duplicated more and runs through your team faster than the good stuff.

Maxim #12
Always have the goal in view

In graduate school we were taught to work from a framework of having the end constantly in view. This is the same philosophy you and I must have as leaders. Think about it: Who builds a house without a blueprint? Who starts a business without a plan? Who goes on a long road trip with no direction or real destination? (Well maybe some people just get in the car and drive, but most don't!)

We should always keep the end in view. What is it that you are looking to accomplish? What should be the end result of a particular project your group is taking on?

Keeping the end in view gives focus and inspiration when things within your organization go "crazy." And this does happen from time to time. Keeping the goal in view will help you recalibrate when things go back to "normal."

Maxim #13
Invest in people; build healthy relationships

The largest and best investment an organization can make is not in a building, a new computer system or research and development, but it's in people.

The network marketing industry has this maxim as its mainstay. Almost every company in that industry believes that their net worth is their network. You may meet some people in the network marketing industry that believe this means using people to get what you want. That is not the stance that I am taking here.

People are the center point of every business or team. Who are you selling your product or service to? Who is your organization attempting to assist? Who works along with you on the team to fulfill the team's goals? The answer to each of those questions is, you guessed it, people.

This is why I believe it is vital to invest in people and healthy relationships for both internal and external purposes.

Internally, you want to invest in building healthy relationships. People tend to function better when they find a common thread with others they work with. In addition, people will follow those who show concern about them.

Vince Lombardi, championship winning NFL coach said it best, "Coaches who can outline plays on a blackboard are a dime a dozen. The ones who succeed are those who get inside their players and motivate them."

Lombardi understood that in order to gain success for his team, he had to make a genuine investment in people, particularly the people on his team.

Externally, you want to make the same investment in people and in building healthy relationships. We have seen in recent times with the unfortunate domestic violence issues, how it has scarred large organizations like the NFL. The only way to repair this is to make investments in people. We saw the same thing a few years before in 2010 with the oil spill in the Gulf of Mexico. When we forget to build healthy relationships with people, our mistakes are always more devastating.

When healthy relationships are forged, it helps to limit the blow when organizations of any size make mistakes.

Maxim #14
Take faith-filled risks

Most for-profit and non-profit companies forget their DNA and they play it safe in an attempt to protect their bottom line and image. Don't rest on your laurels and your previous success. That was yesterday. Today is a new day and tomorrow, if you're fortunate to see it, will bring its own challenges.

I know that you aren't comfortable because it's something new. I know there is a chance that something will go wrong. I know that some of your colleagues won't like it, but you have to find the wherewithal to shake things up a bit and take the risk.

The company, team or group you currently lead was formed by someone, or a group of people taking a faith-filled risk. That is what many organizations and leaders forget.

What opportunities do you see to move your organization further than it currently is? What problems do you see that your organization can reasonably intervene, fix or eliminate?

What is eating at you on the inside; what's that something you need to do? The answer to these questions will be what isolates the faith-filled risk you are in a position to take.

Everyone that revolutionized something had to take a risk. Think about Steve Jobs, Dr. Martin Luther King, Jr., Martin Luther, the German professor of theology and a host of others. Each of these individuals took a faith-filled risk and came out with a great accomplishment.

Will the road be a little rough? Yes it will. Will there be times where you second guess the decision you made? Yes there will. Will you be looked up to by your colleagues with apprehension? Yes you probably will. Now that those questions have been answered what are you waiting for? Identify the risk you are looking to take and take that risk.

Maxim #15
Be accountable

Accountability is a key for any leader. When a leader has been in a position for some time and the organization is successful, he or she sometimes becomes "too big to fail."

This should never be the case for any leader in any organization. No leader is "too big to fail."

There should be a chain of accountability throughout the organization, team or group you lead. Let's look at it closer. The people whom you lead are accountable to you as the leader. To whom is the leader directly accountable?

In the context of a company, there is usually an organization chart which clearly shows who reports to who. Suppose you are at the top of the organization chart -- who are you accountable to? Is it the public you serve? Is it some type of Board?

If there is no accountability in place, I suggest that you as the leader make yourself accountable to someone or to a small group of people. This will not only help you to stay out of trouble personally but it will encourage your organization to paint inside the lines.

When you select the individual or group of people to be accountable to, please select people who are objective and stern. You don't want a bunch of "yes men" or "yes women" as the individual or group you are accountable to. In fact, I suggest an accountability partner or group in all walks of life – business, marriage, etc. It will help you tremendously.

Show me an organization that has no accountability and I will show you an organization that is chaotic and susceptible to fraud and litigation.

Maxim #16
Build team that's smarter and more apt than you

When you look to add a member to your team you want to add the best person for the open position. Insecure leaders pick a "B" or "C" person to fill a position that is critical to the organization. Secure leaders seek those who are sharper than themselves. Secure leaders recognize that placing an "A" person in an open position within the organization has intrinsic value; it has a natural fit.

Insecure leaders don't add members to the team who are smarter than they are for several reasons. First, the smart person is deemed by the leader as a threat to his or her position. Second, the current leader doesn't want to face the possibility of being outperformed by the smarter person. Third, the level of accountability that will come in reverse manner (from the workforce up to leadership) is something the leader doesn't want to deal with.

Each of these reasons say more about the maturity of the leader than the organization's desire to bring in the best qualified person or the intangibles of the potential addition to the team. Leaders who are not developing themselves won't truly challenge their teams to grow and they would never bring on anyone smarter than themselves.

There are many benefits to bringing someone in who is smarter than the leader. First, bringing in a sharp person will typically bring the areas of weakness on a team or in an organization to light. Sharp people tend to find the weak spots where an organization can be vulnerable. Sometimes this occurs by accident and sometimes it doesn't. Nevertheless, the organization can benefit if this is identified and properly used.

Second, everyone on the team can learn something from a sharp person. Having this new information may boost team morale and team unity.

Third, it can make your organization operate more efficiently. If your team is smarter than you, it leaves you time to handle other matters that pertain to your organization. You can leverage the time you have been spending in the day-to-day and develop other ways to move the organization forward.

Fourth, when you are secure as the leader, it is virtually impossible for you to look bad. As the leader, be confident in what you are doing and lead your team appropriately. Don't look at a person smarter than you as a threat; see it as an opportunity to grow.

Maxim #17
Have vision

A leader must have vision – the ability to see how things will be before they actually are that way.

This goes along with Maxim #12 -- keeping the end in view. If developing new leaders is the lifeblood of an organization, then vision is the fuel for the engine. Without vision, it is virtually impossible for an organization or an individual to succeed.

Super Bowl winning coach Tony Dungy says this about vision, "The first step toward creating an improved future is developing the ability to envision it. Vision will ignite the fire of passion that fuels our commitment to do whatever it takes to achieve excellence. Only vision allows us to transform dreams of greatness into the reality of achievement through human action. Vision has no boundaries and knows no limits. Our vision is what we become in life."

Vision also has to do with the ability to take what you are seeing and bring it through the tunnel of dreams and inspiration, making it a reality. That means you must be able to develop a plan to bring it through the tunnel.

Here is a good jumpstart on pulling that idea through the tunnel. Think about these questions: What are you seeing? How do you make it a reality? How long do you think it will take for what you're seeing to be real? What is the first step to getting it done? What are the proceeding steps? Are you developed enough to bring the idea through the tunnel? If you aren't developed enough, what skills or resources are needed to do so? Is your team positioned to assist in bringing this vision to reality? Have you effectively communicated your vision to the members on your team?

If you are a part of a larger organization then you will need a vision that is somewhat aligned with the "mother" organization's vision. Otherwise there may be a conflict of interest. This is something you want to consider and be aware of.

Maxim #18
Develop "thick skin"

The role of leader can cause you to go down some lonely roads. It will also test every fiber of patience and self-control inside of you. Therefore, you must develop thick skin. Many of the challenges that unnerve leaders are minimal, but at the time seem major.

Here are some things that we can do to develop thick skin:

Engage your faith – our faith can keep us grounded through the toughest of times. It is a fact that it takes supernatural strength and power to combat the issues that many leaders deal with on a regular basis. I have found that my faith in God has been the most sustaining attribute in dealing with all of the pressures that come along with being a leader.

Maintain healthy relationships – having a core group of family and friends to fall back on in turbulent times can help as well. Family and friends can make you laugh, cry, think about the situation differently and reinforce your faith.

Manage your memories – remember the times when you faced difficult situations before, the ones that seemed absolutely unbearable. You survived those situations and thus you will survive this one.

Keep your emotional tank full – Go back and read Maxim #4 again, as this is vitally important to developing thicker skin.

<u>Seek counseling</u> – some leaders need the assistance of a counselor to help process things that occur along the leadership journey. In fact, I encourage you to attend counseling periodically. Leaders experience so much, which can cause them to become numb to certain situations. A counselor will allow you to process your emotions correctly and help you separate the "job" or the "office" from home.

As you can see, when I am describing how to have tough skin it never speaks to how you respond to others. It has more to deal with how you respond to situations, more about your mental state. That is what I mean by having thick skin. You don't have to be tough; no one likes a tough guy or gal. You can still be tenderhearted but be tenacious internally.

Maxim #19
Understand the 80/20 Rule

If you have never heard of *Pareto's Principle* or the *80/20 Rule* you may want to enhance your library. The *80/20 Rule* in an organization basically means that 20% of the people within the organization do the majority of the work, while the remaining 80% do less of the work.

When you understand this rule you will be able to manage and understand your organization better. Read up on this principle. I have found it to be true or very close to true.

Maxim #20
Embrace change

Change is inevitable. There is nothing we can ultimately do about it therefore we must embrace it.

Leaders who are maturing understand that change is inevitable. People leave the organization, times change, the methods in which we reach people change. Everything changes.

While leading a youth ministry division of my church, this maxim became so real to me. We had an exceptional group of youth that we were working with. Over the course of three years all of the students went away to college except for a few. What happened? We were back at square one because youth ministry is one of those things that constantly changes.

You can't fight change. I guess you could but it would be a waste of time and effort that could cost your organization dearly. It was the inability to embrace change that forever altered the existence of *Blockbuster*, the now bankrupt media retailer. If you are planning for your organization to grow then you must expect and embrace change.

Change isn't isolated to organizations, it also involves individuals. As you engage in developing yourself as a leader, you will find that your attitude towards certain things will change, your responses will change and ultimately the way you lead will change. You can't stay the same way as a leader; you should be constantly developing.

Entrepreneur, Jim Rohn captured change in the leadership role accurately in this statement, "You must take personal responsibility. You cannot change the circumstances, the seasons, or the wind, but you can change yourself. That is something you have charge of." As a leader, be dedicated to change – changing yourself by constant development.

Maxim #21
Manage blind spots

Blind spots in leadership are equivalent to blind spots to the driver of a car. There are certain things that you can't see from the position you are sitting in. Therefore it is sometimes difficult to make an accurate judgment on the next move for the organization. I don't believe any of us can totally eliminate blind spots but we can manage or limit them.

The Executive White Paper Series of 2012 written by Allen Sockwell and Brad Westveld is a good read as it shows the top ten leadership blind spots.

Hire a coach – world-class athletes have coaches and a world-class leader like you also needs a coach. Phil Jackson coached arguably two of the best NBA athletes in basketball history. What did Phil Jackson bring that made these athletes that much better? He brought perspective and a fresh eye.

Phil Jackson was able to communicate to both Michael Jordan and Kobe Bryant little tips that would make them better athletes and better ballplayers. Mr. Jackson helped both players achieve their full potential.

A business coach should do the exact thing for you. He or she will help you to achieve your full potential by using an assortment of methods to get you there.

Assess – Take an assessment of your blind spots. There are several psychological assessments on the market that are able to do this. The assessment will spot your tendencies and strengths, then it will explain the downside of your strengths.

Go against the grain – I have often heard leaders encourage other leaders to play to their strengths. Each time I hear this I cringe and hope that this advice is not taken.

Although this may be good advice in the perfect situation, life has a habit of exposing your weaknesses and diminishing your strengths.

Why not go against the grain by identifying the areas of weakness and begin strengthening those areas of weakness? You and your team will be better for it. It's okay to have a weakness, we all do. But it isn't okay not to work to strengthen those areas of weakness.

<u>Check with the Cabinet</u> – Leadership can bring great stress to an individual who's trying to figure out the right move when key decisions need to be made. That is a ton of pressure on one person. What if you don't have all of the information? What if there was something so simple that was right there and you missed it? These are the questions that some leaders ask themselves.

Here is what I suggest, create a Cabinet of trusted and knowledgeable individuals who can help you make key decisions. I believe when there are a number of trusted and knowledgeable advisors then a decision can be made in safety.

Learn to lean on these advisors to present you with more information so that ultimately you can make a better decision. Every good leader has a Cabinet.

Maxim #22
Commit to continued education

Many professions have a mandatory continuing education model such as medical professionals, attorneys, education professionals and accountants to name a few. Why is that the case?

These industries understand that things are constantly changing and individuals who are advisors need to be properly informed before something fatal occurs due to bad advice.

In the same fashion, leaders should be committed to continued education. No, you don't have to go back to school! However, I would suggest attending conferences, workshops, webinars and reading books to stay on top of the fresh perspectives out there for your industry and leadership overall.

Leaders are committed to learning. Learning never stops for top leaders.

Maxim #23
Find a mentor

This maxim goes along the lines of hiring a coach as in Maxim #21. Every leader needs someone to be their mentor. They also need a peer mentor and the leader should have someone who they are mentoring. Here is what that looks like and how it should function:

You should have a mentor, hopefully in the same field as you are leading, who is older than you and has more experience than you. This is important because this person, if willing to help, can guide you around many of the pitfalls awaiting you on your leadership journey. They have been where you are trying to get to. They have made the mistakes that you are about to make. Why not learn from someone who has been there before?

Throughout my life I have had mentors. Some of the mentors were with me through pivotal points in my life. Then there were other times, as I got older, when I had to reach out to them for advice in several areas of life.

Now that you have acquired a mentor who is older than you, it is a good idea to find a mentor who is around your age and level of experience. There is a need for relevance within today's industry, camaraderie, encouragement and teamwork.

I have a very good friend who works in one of the same industries as I do. When either one of us gets stumped with an issue as it relates to that industry, we collaborate. It is good to have contemporaries in the same industry working together to help one another. I know it is rare, but if you can find someone like that, it will help you tremendously.

Developing the next generation is something dear to my heart. Because of this, I suggest you find someone younger than you to mentor. Help them to learn what you do. Maybe they will become interested in what you do.

Remember our greatest investment is investing in the lives of others.

Maxim #24
Be a great cheerleader

The late Nelson Mandela said, "It is better to lead from behind and to put others in front, especially when you celebrate victory when nice things occur. You take the frontline when there is danger. Then people will appreciate your leadership."

Corporate America and western civilization have cultured us to be centered on our needs, our achievements first, that of our families a close second (ok maybe 1A) and everyone else after. This is something I would like to challenge you to change.

A great way to get positive energy to flow through your organization is that if you as the leader become the team's greatest cheerleader. This will help build a culture of openness and friendship throughout the organization.

I am not talking about being fake, but authentically being proud that the members of your team are a part of your team. When a member of the team does something great, cheer them on. This activity by you might cost the member a few "dings" at the water cooler but in the long run it will inspire the entire team to accomplish more.

Try to cheer on the members of your team for the next 30 days. I am sure your team will begin to accomplish more as a team than they did in the previous 30 days.

Maxim #25
Delegate to operate

In order for the organization to operate at its optimal capacity it is important to know which tasks to handle, which fires to put out yourself and what to delegate to others.

Here is a thought: Start by delegating tasks that you are not good at or that take a great deal of your time to execute. If you have a sharp person on your team who is capable of accomplishing the task at hand, then you may want to delegate that task.

Please be careful not to delegate tasks that are crucial to the long-term success of the organization.

Do not delegate tasks that contain sensitive information (i.e. pay rates, personal profiles, etc.) You may want to handle those areas or closely oversee them.

Delegating can go a long way toward allowing your team to grow. By delegating, you give the team a sense that you trust them to accomplish a particular task. Delegating also can help you develop your team. Try giving out small tasks in the beginning then tasks that require a bit more work later. You will be amazed what you will learn about your team by doing this.

Maxim #26
Build systems

In order for an organization to grow, it must have the proper infrastructure to sustain its growth. That infrastructure should be developed from the inception of the organization.

When building systems, there are two things that you want to keep in mind. First, think about your day-to-day operations. Write down all of the things that should happen during the day, leave nothing out.

Second, you want to think about problems and how you will solve those problems. This is also something you want to document. You may want to ask a colleague to look over your notes or hire an outside professional to document your processes.

The idea of documenting your processes is so that each person in the organization you lead has a clear role. When everyone knows what they should be doing, it is clearly communicated and followed up by documentation. There are no excuses for sloppy execution.

Systems allow almost anyone to identify what it is they should be doing and how they should be doing it. Network marketing companies do well with systems. Each network marketing company has a set of core components that will almost guarantee success over time for almost anyone.

Systems will also take some of the pressure off leaders. Effective systems will allow the leader to maximize his or her time. The leader will spend less time putting out small fires and can give more time to moving the organization forward with adequate systems in place.

I am a big sports fan and I remember the St. Louis Rams, an NFL franchise, once being called "the greatest show on turf" between 1999 and 2001. Until that time the NFL had no witness an offense as potent as theirs. This offense was anchored by their star running back, Marshall Faulk.

There was a point when Faulk was injured and couldn't play for a stretch of three or four games. One would think during that times, an offense so dependent on Faulk would falter. In fact the team's offense stayed consistent with its previous results, as if Faulk was never injured, because his backup performed well.

The point is the St. Louis Rams' offensive system performed the way any other successful team or organization should. When one of its key contributors is down, things do not fall apart because there is a system in place.

Keep this in mind. If the organization or team dies with the leader's demise or departure it is because adequate systems weren't in place.

Maxim #27
Trust your training

Some people believe that leadership is innate while others believe leadership is a skill that is developed over time. In either case, you have to trust the tools you have whether these were innately received or received by life experience. Whether you believe leadership is innate or learned it is a fact that leaders are designed to lead.

You must trust the training you have received and the training you are currently receiving through your commitment to continued education.

This doesn't mean that you know everything. It doesn't mean that you will never need any help. But it does mean that you should stand confidently in your position, fully secure that you are the person for this leadership assignment for this time in history.

Learn to trust the ability that you have been given. Don't be overconfident but trust your training.

Maxim #28
Leverage technology

Technology has caused our world to change greatly. There seems to be an application for everything. It is wise to leverage technology in some ways to make life and work easier. Embrace the new waves of technology. Let's face it -- technology will only advance, it's not going anywhere. We should never allow technology to completely replace our interactions with our teams, stakeholders and customers. But we must embrace technology and learn to use it to enhance what we do.

There are thousands of smartphone and tablet apps along with tons of programs on the market. Many of the programs and apps will help to increase productivity. Don't be fearful to explore, experience and benefit from the apps and programs that will assist you and your organization.

Maxim #29
Be a people person, not a people pleaser

Every leader wants to be liked whether they admit it or not. There is nothing wrong with being liked but to what extent will you go in order to be liked?

You were called to lead and care for people. Your job as the leader is not to please them. Even in the for-profit context when you have shareholder interest at stake, you aren't there to please people.

I have seen so many leaders resist making correct choices for the sake of avoiding the ridicule of people. Never be pressured by the crowd.

Maxim #30
Be congruent

The word congruent is defined by the Merriam Webster Dictionary as matching or in agreement with something. As a leader, you want to be sure that what you say and ask others to do is congruent with what you are doing.

The worst thing for any team or organization is to have a leader whose verbal instructions greatly differ from their physical execution. This type of behavior will kill morale within the organization. It may cause team members to no longer trust your leadership.

Leaders aren't perfect but allow your "yes" to be "yes" and your "no" to be "no." Whatever you say that you are going to do, do it to the best of your ability.

Maxim #31
Balance Confidence and Arrogance

When we look at the definitions of both words they appear to be pretty close. Arrogance is defined by the Merriam Webster's Dictionary as an attitude of superiority manifested in an overbearing manner or in presumptuous claims or assumptions. Confidence is defined by the same dictionary as a feeling or consciousness of one's powers or of reliance on one's circumstances or the quality or state of being certain.

As a leader is very easy for our confidence in who we are and what we do to be misunderstood as arrogance. We have to learn to balance the two for the greater good of getting our teams to accomplish the mission at hand. In order to manage your confidence you must do three things:

(1) Be realistic about your abilities, your team and the project. Remember if you are recruiting a team more apt than you, rewards for accomplishment are because of the team. You may be the "all-star" but your victories are always because of the team.

(2) Be sure to always give the team credit. Never accept accomplishments that were because of your team without acknowledging your team!

(3) Listen to critiques. At times even in laughter truth is being revealed. Listen to critiques as some of what you are hearing may be true. Ask people to ask you tough questions. You may even want to ask your team to critique you.

(4) Grieve your losses. Remember the times when you failed. As leaders we have all failed at one time or another. If we remember that we aren't perfect, our team isn't perfect and sometimes we will fail, our confidence won't turn into arrogance.

(5) Modesty is the best way. One of my mentors taught me to undersell and over deliver. What he meant by that was to never make too many waves in relation to your pedigree, talent, etc. Instead of making waves, he taught to produce or serve well. This is something I try to instill an each team I lead. Anyone can talk about it, but how many are actually doing it?

Maxim #32
Productivity Is the By-Product of Preparation

Steve Nash, former two-time NBA MVP once said, "You have to rely on your preparation. You got to really be passionate and try to prepare more than anyone else, and put yourself in a position to succeed, and when the moment comes you got to enjoy, relax, breathe and rely on your preparation so that you can perform and not be anxious or filled with doubt."

We can only hope to produce or serve to the ability we have prepared. Preparation is the key to success and productivity. Preparation should be taken seriously because when you don't prepare then the door for failure swings open wider.

My advice to you is to prepare well, be on top of your game at all times, trust your training and produce. You can do it because you have been prepared for it.

Maxim #33
The Law of Cumulative Effect

This is the one law that all leaders must understand. Cumulative effect is simply the compound impact of an individual or organization's decisions and practices over time. This is very powerful.

While leading a team, group or organization you are constantly creating culture whether you know it or not. If you schedule meetings and consistently show up late to these meeting, it is safe to say the result, or cumulative effect, of your actions will most likely be the members of your team will do the same.

Cumulative effect can be found in all walks of life. For instance, the cumulative effect of investing in the stock market over time is that your investment will generate revenue. The cumulative effect of consistent exercise and "clean" eating is weight loss, greater health and positive self-esteem.

Whatever trouble your business, organization or team has previously experienced can be overcome by taking the right action over time. You can begin on the cumulative effect journey today. Here is the challenge to the great leader in you.

Think of something you want to change on your team, organization or even your family. For the next thirty days do something each day to impact positive change in that specific area. After the initial thirty days have passed measure the change and begin again on another thirty day journey until the desired change is apparent. It might take some time to see the change but "stay the course" and you will see dramatic results. It is also a good idea to sit with your coach or mentor to develop the daily steps for the specific area you selected.

Maxim #34
Don't Live In Denial, Identify It and Manage It!

There are far too many leaders who live in denial. I have never understood the reason why we don\t admit the obvious. If there is something that is going wrong within your group, team or organization identify it. It is only after identifying the issue that a solution can suggested or some attempt to manage the situation can be developed.

As the leader you are responsible for what happens to the team and on the team. If the team is doing well you will be congratulated. If the team is not doing well, you will be blamed. John Maxwell captured this concept best when he stated that "everything rises and falls and falls on leadership."

Don't lose hope because of this. As the leader, in most cases, you are able to reverse anything that is going wrong within the organization. Be sure to identify issues within your team or organization quickly and develop a strategy to manage it immediately.

Maxim #35
Don't neglect taking care of yourself

Leaders at times, have the tendency to assist other but neglect care for themselves. Be sure to take care of your self during your leadership journey.

This means monitor your mental health. Leaders need counseling at times to assist in managing all the elements of life and the stresses of leadership. Your mentor or coach can assist with this but you may need to seek out a professional counselor.

Take care of your physical health. Be sure to exercise and eat "clean." According to a study done by the Mayo Clinic, thirty to sixty minutes of regular exercise can lower your blood pressure by 4 to 9 millimeters of mercury.

Enjoy life, don't be so busy leading your team, organization or group that you forget about your friends and family. If you are leader with a family, you have a responsibility to the members of your family. Take some time out of your schedule to enjoy them and be a family!

Ensure that you take a vacation, even if you don't go away, unplug. Turn off your cell phone, check out of social media sites, ban yourself from the Internet and simply relax. You are allowed to do that every once in a while.

Maxim #36
Add to your library often

There is a saying that "leaders are readers". I believe this is true. This is why I am going to give you a book list to start with that contains titles that, I believe, are great for leaders to read. Please understand that this is not an exclusive list but it will serve as a great starting point. In addition to this book, here is the list (in no particular order):

- Good to Great by Jim Collins
- The 21 Irrefutable Laws of Leadership by John C. Maxwell
- Good to Great & the Social Sectors by Jim Collins (great for non-profit leaders)
- The 5 Levels of Leadership: Proven Steps to Maximize Your Potential by John C. Maxwell
- The 7 Habits of Highly Effective People by Stephen R. Covey
- Developing the Leaders Within You by John C. Maxwell
- How To Win Friends & Influence People by Dale Carnegie
- The Five Dysfunctions of a Team by Patrick Lencioni
- Good Leaders Ask Great Questions by John C. Maxwell

- Leadership 101 by John C. Maxwell and Sean Runnette
- Strengths Based Leadership: Great Leaders, Teams, and Why People Follow by Tom Rath and Barry Conchie

Maxim #37
"Gameplan", But Be Open To Audible

The late William "Bill" Walsh, the legendary San Francisco 49ers head coach and the inventor of the West Coast offense was a master game planner. Walsh entered every game with a list of twenty to twenty five plays that his offense would run no matter what. Walsh used these scripted plays to set the tone for the game.

We can learn from Walsh. Leaders should be prepared for every meeting with a game plan. Develop an agenda for the meeting if you are hosting the meeting. If you aren't hosting the meeting, request an agenda.

Agendas guard against meetings being a waste of time. But with all of that being said, don't be afraid to audible – substitute a plan for your original game plan. Sometimes it is necessary to audible. As you continue on your leadership journey you will get a better sense of when to audible and when not to audible.

Maxim #38
Communicate Well and Often

Above all things that must be developed in you as a leader, is the ability to communicate. All leaders must learn to communicate well. Oratory and writing skills help but that isn't the only way to communicate to your team. You must discover the best way to communicate effectively with your team.

It possible, and highly likely, that several people can hear the same information but interpret it differently. I once had a meeting with a team I was leading and found this to be true. Here is what I did:

Everyone received a blank sheet of paper and was asked to close their eyes and listen to my instructions. My first instruction was to fold the paper in half and then to fold it in half again. The next instruction was to tear of the upper right corner, then the lower left corner. The team followed these instruction exactly. (By the way, I performed the exercise while giving instruction)

Surprisingly when everyone opened their eyes and unfolded their pages, everyone's results were different from the page I had. Everyone's paper should have looked the same. What went wrong?

The exercise showed that communication isn't simply giving instruction and executing the instruction. When that occurs the results vary. Effective communication is two sided. The person giving the instruction gives precise instruction.

Instead of simply instructing the team to fold the paper in half, a more effective way to communicate would be to instruct the team to fold the paper in half by folding the bottom of the page toward the top of the page. This would have allowed for everyone to fold the page in the same manner.

The listener should ask questions if something that is being communicated isn't clear. Someone on the team should have asked which way should they fold the page.

Leaders should seek ways to effectively communicate and communicate with your team as much as possible. When there is effective communication within the team or organization everyone is clear on their roles and responsibilities. This is important for teams and organizations of any size.

Maxim #39
Limit Stress By Managing Well

There is one thing that I learned quickly during my leadership journey – get control early. Leadership brings its own challenges and stresses. In order to be effective in your leadership role I suggest that you limit you stress by managing your time and finances well.

When I was younger with less responsibility I was able to remember everything. Over time more responsibility came and I realized that I needed to develop a schedule. One of my mentors said something that was simple yet profound.

The simple yet profound statement was "I would rather have a short pencil rather than a long memory." It was this statement that caused me to develop a schedule and take notes during meetings.

From that day forward I developed a calendar. Before you agree to a meeting check your calendar. Make sure you have enough time to communicate at each meeting. Also make sure you take notes at the meeting. Remember, as your responsibilities increase the more you will need to rely on note taking and scheduling.

In your schedule make sure that you make time for family / friends, a hobby or social activity, meditation or prayer. The leadership position can be very demanding and can get the best of you.

Now that you will begin taking notes and developing a schedule, we move to the next area – finance. Finances can be a huge cause for stress in some leadership positions. Learn to live life on a budget. If you aren't sure how to form a budget please pick up my book entitled, Project Debt Free. Project Debt Free will explain all that you need to know about forming a personal budget.

Leadership is great but make sure that you manage your time and finances well and thus limit your stress.

Maxim #40
Seek Out Win-Win Solutions

When working with people, it is a good practice to seek win-win situations whenever possible. In order to seek out win-win solutions when making decisions you must consider three components: (1) the stakeholders, (2) what needs to be done and (3) cumulative effect.

Stakeholders are all the parties involved in a particular situation. Each set of stakeholders sees things differently and usually does have the win-win idea in the forefront of their thinking.

With regard to what needs to done, a few things must be considered:

(1) How long would you like the task needed to take?
(2) How integral is this particular task?

(3) To what degree can you concede to each stakeholder in order for everyone to win without sacrificing the quality of the product or service you offer?

(4) Do you have equity in the relationships with the stakeholders?

Leaders at times have a certain amount of equity with stakeholders depending on previous experience with the stakeholder. Sometimes this equity comes from the stakeholders based on an intangible quality the stakeholders sees in the leader.

If you have positive equity with some or all of the stakeholders due to past experience with them that is cumulative effect at work. If you don't have positive equity then you must consider the cumulative effect of your decision in any given situation.

This is the tension caused at times when you are in a leadership role. When you seek win-win solutions, stakeholders usually appreciate that. Remember you decisions will have a cumulative effect on your team or organization going forward.

Let's use a manufacturing company which produces shirts as a hypothetical example.

The stakeholders are the company executives, the workers, retail buyer and the end user or purchaser. The end user wants a high quality moderately priced product. The workers typically want an economy effective salary. The retail buyer seeks a good quality product at a reasonable wholesale rate. While the company executives are seeking a high quality product produced at the lowest rate possible.

As you can see each set of stakeholders have a significantly different goal. As the leader here how do you seek out a win-win for all of the stakeholders?

If you were to sacrifice the quality of the product for the sake of watching the bottom line will the end user, retailer buyer and workers be happy? If you pay an economy effective rate to the workers without forsaking the quality of the product, you may upset the retailer buyer and end user because of pricing. What do you do?

This is the tension that leaders face from time to time. The truth is in cases like this, there is no correct answer. Leaders at times while seeking out win-win solutions won't be able to. Sometimes hard decisions have to made that won't allow everyone to "win." Your job as the leader is to seek these win-win opportunities out and execute them if possible.

Maxim #41
Unpopular and Hard Decisions

This leads us into the last maxim of this book. As a leader you will have to make hard decisions at times. These hard decisions will not always cause you to be the most popular person in the office. These hard decisions will also at times cause some of the members of the team to second guess your decisions, it is inevitable. Don't lose heart when this happens. Understand that this is a part of leadership.

Now go, learn, enjoy life, invest in people and lead well!

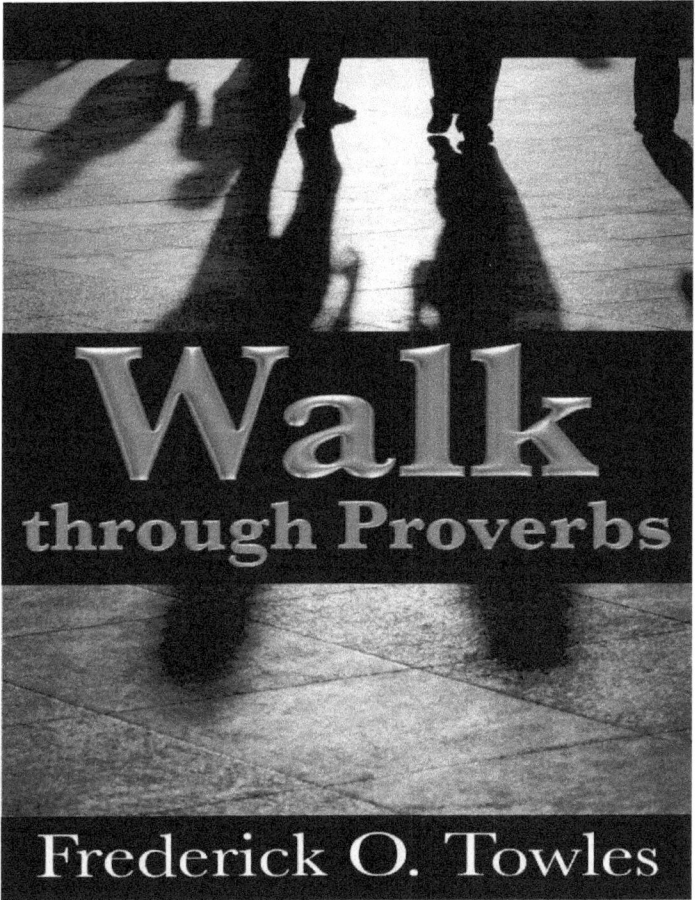

Walk
through Proverbs

Frederick O. Towles

Walk Through Proverbs is a journey through the book of Proverbs containing thought provoking questions, and an invitation to journal through the book of wisdom. For four months, this book will give you daily inspiration and practical application straight from scripture, and to your heart.

FREDERICK TOWLES

PROJECT DEBT FREE

A PRACTICAL GUIDE TO FINANCIAL FREEDOM

Project Debt Free explains the culture of debt in America, highlights the reason for your money troubles, and provides a realistic plan for successfully becoming debt free. While this plan will not get you out of debt overnight, it outlines steps to put you on the road to debt freedom - and keep you on that road.